D0123639

"Freely you have received, freely give."   Matthew 10:8b

"Come unto me, all you who are weary and burdened, and I will give you rest."   Matthew 11: 28

Acknowledgments

I wish to humbly express my appreciation to Reverend James Keller. Thanks to his expert editing and direction, God's Word may go forth clearly, to those who are willing to receive it. I would also like to express my appreciation to Bob and Pat Pollitt, who assisted me with technical issues with earlier printings of *"Love Letter..."*

As time passed, it became evident that the Anointing of the Holy Spirit was upon this work. From simply hand distributing it locally, to Christians and non Christians alike, the Holy Spirit directed it to eventually make its way to a few different states in the United States. Various missionaries were using it in Evangelistic outreaches here at home and abroad.

As more time passed, God made it very clear to me that *"Love Letter..."* needed to play a greater part in the Great Commission, and "go to the ends of the Earth." (Acts 1:8b) I prayed fervently to God, to expand my borders. (see the prayer of Jabez 1 Chronicles 4:9-10)

God "granted my request," when he inspired Pastors Judy and Arthur Baxter, my dear friends and mentors, to E-Mail me on November 16, 2011. As I read the forwarded message, " Are You Called To Write?" "Publish with a Faith Based Publisher; " I was introduced to Xulon Press. Immediately, I sensed the Holy Spirit nudging me to "live by faith and not by sight." (2 Corinthians 5:7) In obedience to God's Will, I took my fist few steps of faith, to publish *"Love-Letter."*

I wish to express my heartfelt thanks and praise to God, who blessed me with faith, makes all things possible, and ordained this book to come to pass.

Thank you, Pastors Jim Keller, Judy Baxter, and Arthur Baxter, for your guidance, inspiration and support.

It is my humble prayer, that each reader reading this book, receives His precious gift of Salvation, and enjoys a deep and personal relationship with Jesus. May He bless your life, and the life of your loved ones, with His peace and His love.

I delight greatly in the Lord;
     my soul rejoices in my God.
For he has clothed me with the garments of salvation
     and arrayed me in a robe of righteousness,
as a bridegroom adorns his head like a priest,
     and as a bride adorns herself with jewels.

                      Isaiah 61: 10

"No longer will they call you Deserted,
     or name your land desolate.
But you will be called Hephzibah,
     And your land Beulah;
for the Lord will take delight in you,
     and your land will be married.
As a young man marries a maiden,
     so will your sons marry you;
as a bridegroom rejoices over his bride,
     so will your God rejoice over you."

                      Isaiah 62: 4-5

Table of Contents

Introduction xiii
One   You Are My Desire 21
Two   No Greater Love: God's Family Dynamics 28
Three   In His Presence 33
Four   The Naked Truth 39
Five   Bonds of Love..45
Six   A Clean Slate..50
Seven   No Fear: Eternally His 58
Eight   Forever His...64
Nine   Reflections of His Love 71
Ten   R.S.V.P 83
Conclusion 87

Introduction

Communication is a privilege that is so common place; it is undervalued, or simply taken for granted. From a simple conversation, to a telephone call, or an e-mail message, we are used to being connected with each other; consequently, we are very uncomfortable when modes of communication are severed, and there is no one to turn to.

For instance, have you ever been through a major storm, and lost you electricity? All of a sudden the television that was tracking the storm goes blank, and your telephone lines go dead. As time passes, the miniscule amount of gray daylight quickly starts to fade into darkness. Anxious, fearful thoughts begin to plague your mind. What will happen next? Am I in danger? Will I make it through the storm alone? You feel so cut off from everything! The desire to check up on loved ones intensifies; nevertheless, without communication, it is impossible. Fears mount, and prayers ascend to God.

Ah, God, prayer, you are never really alone. There is still Someone to communicate with, who is always ready to listen, to care, and to respond. Faith in God, and being able to communicate with Him is such a privilege. Just imagine, God Almighty, the Creator of the Heavens and the Earth, will listen to you from wherever you are, at any time of day or night. Try that with the President, or some other noted official.

> "This is what the Lord says, he who made the earth,
> the Lord who formed it and established it—the Lord is his name:
> 'Call to me and I will answer you and tell you great and unsearchable
> things you do not know.' "
>
> Jeremiah 33: 2-3

If you humble yourself enough to ask for God's help, He will speak these "great, and unsearchable things" directly to your heart; furthermore, He will guide you and show you the way to go. At first, it may seem like a still, small voice inside of you is nudging you in a certain direction. You may think it is a gut feeling or a prompting. Ironically, since these "promptings" are not your own thoughts, you may have mixed feelings about them. For instance, have you ever been traveling to a familiar place, when suddenly, seemingly out of the blue, you get a strong feeling "telling" you to take a different route, but not know why? God, who does know why, may be sharing a "great and unsearchable thing" with you.

He may be steering you away from impending danger, or arranging a Divine meeting with someone you never planned to meet. On the other hand, He may simply be testing you to see if you are listening and will obey. These are a few examples where you may or may not recognize His voice immediately, however, the more He speaks to you, and the more you listen and obey, the more familiar and welcome His still small voice will be.

> "...How gracious He will be when you cry for help! As soon as he hears, he will answer you. Although the Lord

gives you the bread of adversity and the water of affliction, your teachers will be hidden no more; with your
own eyes you will see them. Whether you turn to the
right or to the left, your ears will hear a voice behind
you, saying, "This is the way; walk in it."

Isaiah 30: 19b – 21

No One wants the "bread of adversity or the "water of
affliction;" yet, these are as much a part of life as prosperity
and peace. Thankfully, we can rely on God to guide us to
the "right or to the left," in the rough and the smooth areas
of life. He did not promise us a care free life; in fact, Jesus
himself states:

"...In this world you will have trouble.
But take heart! I have overcome the world."

John 16:33b

Jesus truly desires to be a part of your life; but, He will
not force himself on you. He would like to help you "overcome the world," and free you from the power of sin. To
receive His forgiveness, guidance, comfort, peace, and ultimate victory over sin, He simply beckons you to come to
Him.

In my teenage years, I accepted Jesus' invitation, and
invited Him into my heart as my personal Lord and Savior.
I humbly confessed my sins to Him, and was instantly forgiven. Because He paid the penalty for my sins with His precious blood when He died on the cross, in exchange for my
sins He gave me His righteousness. Thus, God sees Jesus in
me, not my sins; therefore I am right (righteous) in His sight.

"God made him who had no sin to be sin for us, so that in
him we might become the righteousness of God."

2 Corinthians 5:21

Admittedly, as a human being I am far from perfect; consequently, I have many areas in my life which He is still helping me change. It is comforting to know that while He helps me change from my sinful ways, and grow to be more like Him, my past, present, and future sins are forgiven! Would you like to make this great exchange with The Almighty? He would like to make it with you.

"You were taught, with regard to your former way of life, to put off your old self, which is being corrupted by its deceitful desires; to be made new in the attitude of your minds; and to put on the new self, created to be like God in true righteousness and holiness." Ephesians 4: 22-24

When you have the righteousness of Christ dwelling within you, you are never alone. As He resides in your heart, by the power of the Holy Spirit, you are in constant communion with God. His presence is like a steady and reliable anchor in life; therefore, as you walk together hand in hand through life's journey, thinking about Jesus and giving Him spontaneous praise, worship, and prayer become a way of life.

I seldom pray using memorized prayers. I discovered that by simply reciting memorized words, without really thinking about their meaning, my prayers were ritualistic and empty. You may be thinking, but didn't Jesus Himself give us the Lord's Prayer, in the Gospel of Matthew 6: 9-13? Yes, He certainly did. In the past I used to simply repeat the words of this beautiful prayer, over and over, with little thought; however, now I use these words as a guide, praying them back to Him in adoration, praise, worship and thanksgiving. For instance, "Our Father in heaven" Matthew 6: 9b. Lord, you are not only the Lord of the Universe, you are my father. How awesome! God is my father, and I am his daughter. How I love you. Thank you for your fatherly love and protection... After I pray about God's fatherly qualities and love, I move on to his Holiness. "Hallowed be your name..." Matthew 6:9c. Holy, Holy, Holy are you Lord. There is none like you. Please help me to be holy as you are holy. Lord I need your help in this.... I continue in this way throughout the entire prayer, use everyday language, and speak to God from my heart.

Prayer is very similar to the communication between two very close friends. Not only do they freely share their joys and sorrows, and their wants and needs, but also, they trust and confide in each other, never betraying that trust. They truly enjoy conversing with each other. Similarly, it is important to remember that prayer is a two way conversation with God. So, just as we speak to Him, there will be times when He speaks back to us, in a gentle, but unmistakable way. God would love to speak with you. Would you like to speak with Him?

In this book, I will focus on a particular "conversation" that the Lord shared with me. It was in the mid 1990's, when I was in a hotel on a missionary trip. I woke up very early, and went to the window to look at my wrist watch. As my eyes beheld a beautiful sunrise, peeking over the peaceful blue ocean, I became immediately inspired, sensing unexplainable joy and peace. The presence of God was so strong at that moment, that words cannot explain it. I felt light, carefree, everything seemed perfect. Without trying to form any thoughts of my own, God gave me the thought of a husband and wife on their wedding day, in unsullied perfect love, hugging each other intensely.

Then, He gave me a new thought. This time, instead of the husband and wife hugging each other, I pictured myself as a little girl, hugging Jesus, as He compassionately look down at me and loved me. It was as if Jesus and I were that "perfect" couple. Shortly thereafter, words came rushing into my mind so quickly, I could hardly write them down fast enough.

I quickly took a piece of hotel stationary, and wrote down the words exactly as He gave them to me. I felt like I was taking dictation, writing words that were clear and exact.

When I came home, I shared these words with family and friends, and made a few guest appearances giving my testimony. Hearts were touched. The Holy Spirit was moving in my life and in the lives of many other people. As time passed I went on a few more mission trips, and *Love Letter* seemed to fade into the background for a while.

One morning, while cleaning out a drawer, I stumbled across the scrap paper of *Love Letter*. God immediately put on my heart the desire to do something with this gift, other than store it in my dresser drawer. The desire to write a book came to me. I've never written any other books, so this was a major undertaking. I had to follow the Spirit's lead, not give in to fear or human inadequacy, but simply trust Him to guide me.

After about a year, a booklet form of *Love Letter* came to pass. Many copies were printed, and I prayed fervently for all the people that would eventually receive it. I prayed it would touch hearts and minds, it would change lives, and that souls would be saved. God bountifully answered my prayer; but, the Holy Spirit was not finished yet.

I prayed again for *Love Letter* to reach the ends of the Earth, and for God to abundantly bless each everyone who reads it. The Holy Spirit showed me I needed to have it published to accomplish His Will. Dear reader, in obedience to His leading, you are now reading this book.

In conclusion, I will share with you the words from the Holy Spirit, in *"Love Letter from Jesus."* Come! Refresh yourself with "rivers of living water" and drink at God's oasis. You were included in my prayers long before this book was published. Enjoy your journey through *Love Letter from Jesus: Come to the Savior*. May you enjoy the many Scripture verses, along with a few of my own commentaries as you read *Love Letter*. Come and see what answers to prayer God has in store, just for you!

Love- Letter from Jesus

" My heart yearns to be with you; you are the desire of my heart; I desire to be with you always.

My love for you is greater than you can know. Come, come, come unto Me. Take My hand, come.

Come, let us steal away together, alone, quiet, our hearts and minds one.

Bare yourself before me; don't be ashamed. Nothing about you is hidden from My sight, anyway.

Come close, closer, even closer. Let us join with each other in oneness of body, soul, spirit, and mind.

Pure are you in My sight, for I have cleansed you Myself. You are pure and whole with Me. Don't be afraid.

Fear not, I will be with you always; we are one never to part. My love for you never ends.

Come, come, come unto Me; take My hand. You are Mine forever.

Love Me as I love you. You are Mine forever; come!"

Chapter One

You Are My Desire

A man sees a woman, or a woman sees a man, and the spark of human desire is lit. As they get to know each other, yearnings begin to burn from deep within, and the spark of human love ignites. One may wonder, did desire light out of true, selfless, love for each other, or did it light out of lustful, self-gratifying motives; unfortunately, the latter is usually true.

Fortunately, God's desire to love mankind is quite different. Unlike human love and relationships, based on mutual feelings and emotions toward each other, God's love is not dependent on our feelings toward Him. He continues to love us, despite our feelings, or our sins. Although God hates sin, and is very saddened by our indifference towards Him, He continues to love the sinner with a deep, measureless, selfless, "Agape" love. According to the *American Heritage Dictionary,* "Agape" love is: "Love as revealed in Jesus, seen as spiritual and selfless and a model for humanity. Love that is spiritual, not sexual, in its nature."

"My heart yearns to be with you; you are the Desire of My heart"

Imagine, Jesus revealing His love to us by sharing His heartfelt yearnings and desires to be One with us in Spirit. How deeply He desires to be in fellowship with us; still, He knew that this would be impossible in our sinful state. Knowing that we needed a Savior, because we could not save ourselves, He broke down the wall of sin that separates us from God, and allows us to come to Him through faith.

"But the Scripture declares that the whole world is a prisoner of sin, so that what was promised being given through faith in Jesus Christ might be given to those who believe.
Galatians 3:22

In order to fulfill His promise, and free us from the prison of sin, He paid the penalty for our sins with His precious blood, when He died a painful, sacrificial, death on the cross. Human standards cannot measure the depth and sincerity of Jesus' love; because God is love.

"And so we know and rely on the love God has for us. God is love. Whoever lives in love lives in God, and God in him."
1 John 4:16

"This is how God showed his love among us: He sent his one and only Son into the world that we might live through him. This is love: not that we loved God, but that he loved us and sent his Son as an atoning sacrifice for our sins." 1 John 9-10

"For God so loved the world that he gave his one and only Son, that whoever believes in him, shall not perish, but have eternal life."
John 3:16

"I pray that out of his glorious riches he may strengthen you with power through his Spirit in your inner being, so that Christ may dwell in your hearts through faith. And I pray that you, being rooted and established in love, may have power, together with all the saints, to grasp how wide and long and high and deep is the love of Christ, and to know this love that surpasses knowledge—that you may be filled to the measure of all the fullness of God." Ephesians 3:16-19

"My heart yearns to be with you; you are the desire of my heart."

Jesus is a loving, gentle Savior, who is seeking a deep and precious relationship with you. He yearns to be with you, and you are the desire of His heart. Will you allow Him into your heart?

"Here I am! I stand at the door and knock. If anyone hears my voice and opens the door, I will come in and eat with him, and he with me." Revelation 3:20

"Today, if you hear his voice, do not harden your hearts." Hebrews 4:7b

"For the Lord takes delight in his people; he crowns the humble with salvation."

"The Lord your God is with you, he is mighty to save. He will take great delight in you, he will quiet you with his love, he will rejoice over you with singing." Zephaniah 3:17

It is simple and easy to come to Jesus; although, at times, mankind tends to make simple things very complicated. For instance, some people have difficulty admitting they were wrong; therefore, they place the blame on others, or on circumstances. This natural tendency began back in the Garden of Eden, when Adam and Eve disobeyed God, by eating the forbidden fruit. When confronted by God, they were fearful of the consequences of their sins, and passed the blame off to each other, and to Satan.

"But the Lord called to the man, "Where are you?" He answered, "I heard you in the Garden, and I was afraid because I was naked; so I hid."   Genesis 3:9-10

" And he said, "Who told you that you were naked? Have you eaten from the tree that I commanded you not to eat from?"   Genesis 3:11

"The man said, "The woman you put here with me–she gave me some fruit from the tree, and I ate it."   Genesis 3:12

Then the Lord God said to the woman," What is this you have done?" The woman said, "The serpent deceived me, and I ate."   Genesis 3: 13

Unfortunately, this tendency to sin without taking accountability still continues to this day.

Fortunately, God still loves us and earnestly wants to help. He wants us to break this sin and blame cycle with one basic requirement: to admit that we have sinned.

"If we claim to be without sin, we deceive ourselves and the truth is not in us. If we confess our sins, he is faithful and just and will forgive us our sins and purify us from all unrighteousness."   1 John 1: 8-9

Jesus invites us to come to Him Just as we are, in our sinful state. First, we need to admit our sins and humbly confess them to Him. Next, we need to ask for His forgiveness, and we'll be immediately forgiven. We also need to repent, which is a desire to stop willfully sinning. According to the *American Heritage Dictionary*, to "repent" is to "feel such regret for past conduct as to change one's mind regarding it—To make a change for the better as a result of remorse or contrition for one's sins." Spiritually, repentance is a day by day growth process, which God gives us the power to accomplish.

"...continue to work out your salvation with fear and trembling, for it is God who works in you to will and to act according to his good purpose."   Philippians 2:12b-13

"...'restore me, and I will return, because you are the Lord my God. After I strayed, I repented; after I came to understand, I beat my breast. I was ashamed and humiliated because I bore the disgrace of my youth.'"
                                                        Jeremiah 31: 18b-19

"...But unless you repent, you too will all perish."
                                                        Luke 13:3b

"He (God) is patient with you, not wanting anyone to perish, but everyone to come to repentance."   2 Peter 3:9b

After we confess our sins to Jesus and repent of our sinful ways, His grace—God's undeserved, unearned favor, showers over us like a spring rain. He then forgives us, revives us, and gives us a brand new start in life, a clean slate, so to speak.

"Who is a God like you, who pardons sin and forgives the transgression of the remnant of his inheritance? You do not stay angry forever but delight to show mercy. You will again have compassion on us; you will tread our sins underfoot and hurl all our iniquities into the depths of the sea."
                                                        Micah 7: 18-19

Jesus exemplified the perfect model of compassion, and showed His deep awareness and concern for our sinful, suffering state.

"The Lord is compassionate and gracious, slow to anger, abounding in love. He will not always accuse, nor will he harbor his anger forever; he does not treat us as our sins deserve or repay us according to our iniquities."

Psalm 103: 8-10

Being God, and having immeasurably higher standards than any human being, Jesus not only wishes to relieve our sinful state, but also, He provides the way of relief—the forgiveness of sins, on the cross of Calvary.

"Jesus answered, "I am the way and the truth and the life. No one comes to the Father except through me."   John 14:6

"Therefore Jesus said again, "I tell you the truth, I am the gate for the sheep."   John 10:7

"I am the gate; whoever enters through me will be saved."   John 10:9

"The thief comes only to steal and kill and destroy; I have come that they might have life, and have it to the full." "I am the good shepherd. The good shepherd lays down his life for the sheep."   John 10: 10-11

"My heart yearns to be with you…"

Jesus is the Good Shepherd, and we are His sheep. Would you like to share in His great gift of love? If so, He would like to lead you into a new life on Earth, and give you the ultimate promise of eternal life in heaven, forever.

"He calls his own sheep by name and leads them out. When he has brought out all his own, he goes on ahead of them, and his sheep follow him because they know his voice."

John 10: 3b-4

Do you know the voice of Jesus, and follow Him? He is calling you—Come, come unto Me!

Chapter Two

No Greater Love — God's Family Dynamics

J esus, the Good Shepherd, paid the penalty for our sins when he died on the cross in our place. He took the pain and suffering intended for us, upon himself.

"In bringing many sons to glory, it was fitting that God, for whom and through whom everything exists, should make the author of their salvation perfect through suffering. Both the one who makes men holy and those who are made holy are of the same family. So Jesus is not ashamed to call them brothers."   Hebrews 2: 10-11

"Greater love has no one than this, that he lay down his life for his friends. You are my friends if you do what I command."   John 15: 13-14

"My love for you is greater than you can know. Come, come, come unto Me. Take My hand, come."

"He came to that which was his own, but his own did not receive him. Yet to all who received him, to those who believed in his name, he gave the right to become children of God—children born not of natural descent, nor of human decision or a husband's will, but born of God." John 1: 11-13

Have you ever seen a little child run and jump into the arms of his father? Not concerned that his father could drop him, the child simple trusts in the love of the father, to catch him, and protect him from all harm. This is simple, child-like faith—the kind of faith that God expects from His children.

"But Jesus called the children to him and said, "Let the little children come to me, and do not hinder them, for the kingdom of God belongs to such as these. I tell you the truth, anyone who will not receive the kingdom of God as a little child will never enter it."   Luke 18: 16-17

In today's society, the often quoted phrase, "we are all children of God," is not really true. Yes, we are all unique creations of God, and without Him there is no life; however, to be a child of God requires a commitment on our part. Only those who accept Jesus into their hearts as their personal Lord and Savior, and trust in Him, with simple child-like faith, are the true children of God.

"...Jesus declared, " I tell you the truth, no one can see the kingdom of God unless he is born again."   John 3:3b

"How can a man be born when he is old"? Nicodemus asked.
                                                John 3: 4a

"...Jesus answered, "I tell you the truth, no one can enter the kingdom of God unless he is born of water and the Spirit. Flesh gives birth to flesh, but the Spirit gives birth to spirit. You should not be surprised at my saying, ' You must be born again.'"   John 3: 5-7

Being "born again" is not a new religion, or a radical idea; it is a command from Jesus Christ Himself. It refers to a spiritual renewal, which begins deep in the hearts of true believers.

Only with the help of the Holy Spirit, will these inner changes begin to take place, giving these believers the desire and ability to live more Christ-like lives. They will consider God's will in their every day decisions by asking themselves, "What would Jesus want me to do?" The main idea is that living for God, pleasing Him, and putting His desires above our own selfish desires, becomes an integral part of daily living. The Spiritual rebirth is a growth process, which starts the moment Jesus is accepted as Lord and Savior, and continues until physical death.

"Take My hand, come."

"And now, dear children, continue in him, so that when he appears we may be confident and unashamed before him at his coming. If you know that he is righteous, you know that everyone who does what is right has been born of him."

1 John 2: 28-29

"My love for you is greater than you can know."

"How great is the love the Father has lavished on us, that we should be called children of God! And that is what we are!

1 John 3: 1a

"Dear friends, now we are children of God, and what we will be has not yet been made known. But we know that when he appears, we shall be like him, for we shall see him as he is. Everyone who has this hope in him purifies himself, just as he is pure."

1 John 3: 2-3

"Everyone who sins breaks the law; in fact, sin is lawless-ness. But you know that he appeared so that he might take away our sins. And in him is no sin. No one who lives in him keeps on sinning. No one who continues to sin has either seen him or known him."   1 John 3: 4-6

"Dear children, do not let anyone lead you astray. He who does what is right is righteous, just as he is righteous. He who does what is sinful is of the devil, because the devil has been sinning from the beginning. The reason the Son of God appeared was to destroy the devil's work. No one who is born of God will continue to sin, because God's seed remains in him; he cannot go on sinning, because he has been born of God."   1 John 3: 7-9

"Come, come, come unto Me, take My hand. Come."

"Whoever believes in the Son has eternal life, but whoever rejects the Son will not see life, for God's wrath remains on him."   John 3:36

(Jesus speaking) " I tell you the truth, whoever hears my word and believes him who sent me has eternal life and will not be condemned; he has crossed over from death to life."
                                    John 5: 24

Have you decided to believe in Jesus the Son, become a child of God, and enter into His family? Or, will you choose to reject Jesus, and have His wrath remain on you? The choice is yours. Before you decide, remember, your choice will affect you for eternity. Only His children (heirs) become recipients of the benefits of His inheritance— eternal life in Heaven, forever. Where do you want to spend eternity?

Jesus is gently calling you to come, believe, and experi-ence a foretaste of eternal life, right here on Earth. Come;

spend precious time with Him, experiencing His love, peace, joy, and warmth of being in His presence.

Chapter Three

In His Presence

Coming to Jesus, and enjoying a personal relationship with Him, brings great peace. Just the ability to detach from your rushed and hurried pace of life, and bask in His presence, is like finding an oasis while traveling through the desert. The importance of finishing just one more chore, or going to one more store, becomes so unimportant, when you simply stop—stop and spend time at the feet of the Master, Jesus Christ.

The Gospel of Luke describes two sisters, Mary and Martha. Mary was quiet, reflective, and enjoyed spending time sitting in the presence of Jesus, listening to what He had to say. With Him, she felt safe, secure, peaceful, and loved. Martha, on the other hand, was extremely task and service orientated. She placed the utmost importance on completing all the necessary preparations for Jesus' visit. Her mind was swirling with numerous jobs and endless details that needed to be completed—right now. Although it is important to have a clean home and adequate food for a guest, Martha placed too much emphasis on making a good impression on Jesus, rather than being impressed by Him. Both sisters had good personality traits; however, because Martha focused solely on the preparations for the Lord's visit, and not of the Lord himself, she was too busy to visit with him and enjoy his company. This left her empty, dry,and worn out. Consequently, she was frustrated and angry with her sister Mary.

"As Jesus and his disciples were on their way, he came to a village where a woman named Martha opened her home to him. She had a sister called Mary, who sat at the Lord's feet listening to what he said."   Luke 10:38-39

" But Martha was distracted by all the preparations that had to be made. She came to him and asked, "Lord, don't you care that my sister has left me to do the work by myself? Tell her to help me!"   Luke 10:40

"Martha, Martha," the Lord answered, " you are worried and upset about many things, but only one thing is needed. Mary has chosen what is better, and it will not be taken away from her."   Luke 10: 41-42

Have you been feeling empty, dry, frustrated, or angry with you present life style? Are you placing too much importance on doing the next thing or perfecting every detail? Perhaps balancing your family, career, and social obligations is getting overwhelming. If so, like Martha, you are too busy, and need to follow Jesus' advice, and "choose what is better." Why not stop, and sit quietly at the feet of Jesus and listen to Him?

"Come, let us steal away together, alone, quiet, our hearts and minds one."

34

"O God, you are my God, earnestly I seek you; my soul thirsts for you, my body longs for you, in a dry and weary land where there is no water.   Psalm 63:1

"As the deer pants for streams of water, so my soul pants for you, O God. My soul thirsts for God, for the living God. When can I go and meet with God?   Psalm 42: 1-2

Fortunately, God allows us to come and meet with Him—anytime. O, how He is longing for you to come to him.

"Today, if you hear his voice, do not harden your hearts."
                                        Hebrews 4: 7b

Are you "thirsty" for a better relationship with God? Jesus would like to satisfy your thirst.

"Jesus stood and said in a loud voice, "If anyone is thirsty, let him come to me and drink. Whoever believes in me, as the Scripture has said, streams of living water will flow from within him. By this he meant the Spirit whom those who believed in him were later to receive."   John 7: 37b-39a

If you have accepted Jesus into your life as you personal Lord and Savior, His precious Holy Spirit already resides in your heart. You not only have a beautiful union with The Almighty; but also, He gives you the ability to hear His voice.

"Our hearts and minds, one."

"If you love me, you will obey what I command. And I will ask the Father, and he will give you another Counselor to be with you forever—the Spirit of truth. The world cannot accept him, because it neither sees him nor knows him. But you know him, for he lives with you and will be in you.

John 14: 15-17

"But he who unites himself with the Lord is one with him in spirit."

1 Corinthians 6:17

"Because I live, you also will live. On that day you will realize that I am in my Father, and you are in me, and I am in you."

John 14: 19b-20

"Come let us steal away together, alone, quiet."

In a marriage there is a mystical union of two persons becoming one. Nurturing this relationship with open communication, and ample time alone, is of utmost importance. As the relationship grows, thought patterns tend to merge, and spouses can get proficient at understanding and meeting each others' needs. Likewise, nurturing you Spiritual relationship with God through fervent prayer, quiet, uninterrupted time alone with Him, enjoying His presence, and studying the Bible, are of utmost importance for your relationship with God to grow. With God's help, and your continued devotion to Him, you will develop Christ-like thought patterns. So, the more you think like Christ, the more you will act like Him. As you continue to give God first place in your life, He promises to meet all your needs.

"And pray in the Spirit on all occasions with all kinds of prayers and requests."

Ephesians 6:18a

"The prayer of a righteous man is powerful and effective."

James 5:16b

"And my God will meet all your needs according to his glorious riches in Christ Jesus."   Philippians 4: 19

In the Gospel of Matthew 14: 14-24, Jesus shows us how He met the needs of over 5000 people, by miraculously feeding them with only five loaves of bread and two fish. He also shows us that after first meeting the needs of the people, He needed to meet his own needs, and went off to a solitary place to pray. Since Jesus himself needed time alone to pray, to be free from distractions, and to be with His Father, how much more do we need time alone to pray, and do the same?

"Immediately, Jesus made the disciples get into the boat and go on ahead of him to the other side, while he dismissed the crowd. After he had dismissed them, he went up on a mountainside by himself to pray. When evening came, he was there alone..."   Matthew 14: 22-23

"But when you pray, go into your room, close the door, and pray to your Father, who is unseen. Then your Father, who sees what is done in secret, will reward you." Matthew 6: 6

"Our hearts and minds one."

In the Gospel of John 17: 20-23, Jesus prayed for all believers, which includes us today. Just imagine, Jesus was praying for you and for me, before we were born. His prayer expresses the deep, desire of His heart, for our hearts and minds to be one with His, and for us to be in complete unity with God and with each other. After He prayed for his Disciples, Jesus prayed for us:

"My prayer is not for them alone. I pray also for those who will believe in me through their message, that all of them may be one, Father, just as you are in me and I am in you.

May they also be in us so that the world may believe that you have sent me. I have given them the glory that you gave me, that they may be one as we are one: I in them and you in me. May they be brought to complete unity to let the world know that you sent me and have loved them even as you have loved me." John 17: 20-23

"If you have any encouragement from being united with Christ, if any comfort from his love, if any fellowship with the Spirit, if any tenderness and compassion, then make my joy complete by being like-minded, having the same love, being one in spirit and purpose." Philippians 2: 1-2

Being united with Christ, experiencing immeasurable joy and peace, while basking in the comfort of His tender love— what a precious promise. Are you ready to be intimate with the Almighty?

Chapter Four

The Naked Truth

Transparent honesty and openness are essential for relationships to grow and flourish. As you develop a relationship with God, there is no room for deep dark secrets or for hidden sins in your heart. Although you may not want to reveal these sins because of fear or embarrassment, remember, God knows all about them. So, allow Him to search your heart, and confess the sins He points out to you. Then, you can enjoy His forgiveness and His presence.

"Bare yourself before Me, don't be ashamed.
Nothing about you is hidden from My sight, anyway."

"O Lord, you have searched me and you know me. You know when I sit and when I rise; you perceive my thoughts from afar. You discern my going out and my lying down; you are familiar with all my ways. Before a word is on my tongue, you know it completely, O Lord."   Psalm 139: 1-4

"Search me, O God, and know my heart; test me and know my anxious thoughts. See if there is any offensive way in me, and lead me in the way everlasting." Psalm 139: 23-24

"Nothing in all creation is hidden is hidden from God's sight. Everything is uncovered and laid bare before the eyes of him to whom we must give account."   Hebrews 4: 13

"Therefore, since we have a great high priest who has gone through the heavens, Jesus the Son of God, let us hold firmly to the faith we profess. For we do not have a high priest who is unable to sympathize with our weaknesses, but we have one who has been tempted in every way, just as we are—yet was without sin. Let us then approach the throne of grace with confidence, so that we may receive mercy and find grace to help us in our time of need." Hebrews 4: 14-16

Jesus paid the penalty for our sins when He died on the cross; nevertheless, He rose from the dead, ascended into heaven, and sits at the right hand of the Father in Heaven. Consequently, He is always ready to hear our prayers and to intercede for us. Through Jesus we can approach the Father with freedom and confidence. What a great High Priest and Savior we have.

"Now there have been many of those priests, since death prevented them from continuing in office; but because Jesus lives forever, he has a permanent priesthood. Therefore he is able to save completely those who come to God through him, because he always lives to intercede for them."
                                                   Hebrews 7: 23-25

"In him and through faith in him we may approach God with freedom and confidence."   Ephesians 3:12

"Jesus answered, "I am the way and the truth and the life. No one comes to the Father except through me."   John 14:6

"I urge, then, first of all, that requests, prayers, intercession and thanksgiving be made for everyone—for kings and all those in authority, that we may live peaceful and quiet lives in all godliness and holiness. This is good, and pleases God our Savior, who wants all men to be saved and to come to a knowledge of the truth. For there is one God and one mediator between God and men, the man Christ Jesus, who gave himself as a ransom for all men—the testimony given in its proper time."   1 Timothy 2: 1-6

> *"Bare yourself before Me, don't be ashamed."*
> *"Nothing about you is hidden from My sight, anyway."*

Do you have any secret sins that are weighing heavily on your heart? Since God wants everyone to be saved, and He has given us Jesus as our Savior and intercessor, why not bare yourself before Him, confess your sins, and receive forgiveness?

"When I kept silent, my bones wasted away through my groaning all day long. For day and night your hand was heavy upon me; my strength was sapped as in the heat of summer. Then I acknowledged my sin to you and did not cover up my iniquity. I said, "I will confess my transgressions to the Lord"—and you forgave the guilt of my sin."
                          Psalm 32: 3-5

What a privilege we have to come to God—just as we are. Don't be ashamed. After all, He knows all about your sins anyway. Confess you sins. Repent: turn around from you sinful ways. Then you will receive His complete forgiveness. Having done this, you can revel in the perfect peace of His love and bask in His presence.

"I have surely heard Ephraim's moaning: 'you disciplined me like an unruly calf, and I have been disciplined. Restore me, and I will return, because you are the Lord my God. After I strayed, I repented; after I came to understand, I beat my breast. I was ashamed and humiliated because I bore the disgrace of my youth.'"   Jeremiah 31: 18-19

"Is not Ephraim my dear son, the child in whom I delight? Though I often speak against him, I still remember him. Therefore my heart yearns for him; I have great compassion for him," declares the Lord."   Jeremiah 31: 20

"Those whom I love I rebuke and discipline. So be earnest, and repent. Here I am! I stand at the door and knock. If anyone hears my voice and opens the door, I will come in and eat with him, and he with me.   Revelation 3: 19-20

"Blessed is he whose transgressions are forgiven, whose sins are covered. Blessed is the man whose sin the Lord does not count against him and in whose spirit is no deceit."
                    Psalm 32: 1-2

    Yes, the Lord is truly merciful to those who acknowledge their sins and confess them to Him. Are you honest with yourself and with God; or, have you deceived yourself into believing that you are a really good person—just as you are?

"What shall we conclude then? Are we any better? Not at all! We have already made the charge that Jews and Gentiles alike are all under sin. As it is written: "There is no one righteous, not even one; there is no one who understands, no one who seeks God. All have turned away, they have together become worthless; there is no one who does good, not even one."   Romans 3: 9-12

"He who conceals his sins does not prosper, but whoever confesses and renounces them finds mercy. Blessed is the man who always fears the Lord, but he who hardens his heart falls into trouble."   Proverbs 28: 13-14

"If we claim to be without sin, we deceive ourselves and the truth is not in us. If we confess our sins, he is faithful and just and will forgive us our sins and purify us from all unrighteousness. If we claim we have not sinned, we make him out to be a liar and his word has no place in our lives."
                                                                        1 John 1:8-10

"… Bare yourself before Me, don't be ashamed…"

After you confess your sins to Jesus and are forgiven, a precious bonding develops between you and God, and a growth process begins. You become more and more like Jesus as you walk, "in his light." As with any growth process, this takes time and practice. For instance, just as a child crawls, tries to stand, takes a step, falls down, and gets up again with the help of a trusted parent, so it is with Christian growth. The Lord Jesus Christ is always at our side, holding our hand, helping us walk, and picking us up when we fall. Won't you walk in the light of the Lord?

"If the Lord delights in a man's way he makes his steps firm; though he stumble, he will not fall, for the Lord upholds him with his hand."   Psalm 37: 23-24

"This is the message we have heard from him and declare to you: God is light; in him there is no darkness at all. If we claim to have fellowship with him yet walk in darkness, we lie and do not live by the truth. But if we walk in the light as he is in the light, we have fellowship with one another, and the blood of Jesus, his Son, purifies us from all sin."

1 John 1: 5-7

"My dear children, I write this to you so that you will not sin. But if anyone does sin, we have one who speaks to the Father in our defense—Jesus Christ, the Righteous One. He is the atoning sacrifice for our sins, and not only for ours but also for the sins of the whole world." 1 John 2: 1-2

Jesus wants to take away your sins. Did you bare yourself before the eyes of the Almighty? He lovingly calls to you, come; come close to Me.

Chapter Five

Bonds of Love

People who care about each other enjoy being in the other persons' company. One beckons the other to come, and the other joyfully heeds the call. Time spent together is a pleasure, not a duty or a burden. As the relationship grows, a deeper sense of devotion develops. For instance, coming to the other person without being called, devoting yourself, your time and your attention to him or her happens naturally and joyfully. Jesus loves you very deeply, and He is beckoning you to come to Him. Will you heed His call to come, and be devoted to Him?

> *"Come close, closer, even closer. Let us join with each other in body, soul, spirit, and mind."*

"The Lord appeared to us in the past, saying: " I have loved you with an everlasting love; I have drawn you with loving-kindness."   Jeremiah 31:3

"…'I will bring him near and he will come close to me, for who is he who will devote himself to be close to me?'

Declares the Lord." " 'So you will be my people, and I will be your God.'"   Jeremiah 30: 21b-22

People, who truly devote themselves to God, begin to trust Him completely with every detail of their life. They realize to be truly one of His people, He must fully be their God. Consequently, they begin to give Him control of their life, by committing their body, soul, spirit, and mind to Him. They seek God daily for strength and direction.

"Submit yourselves, then, to God. Resist the Devil, and he will flee from you. Come near to God and he will come near to you. Wash your hands, you sinners, and purify your hearts, you double-minded."   James 4: 7-8

"Humble yourselves before the Lord, and he will lift you up."   James 4: 10

"Kiss the Son, lest he be angry and you be destroyed in your way, for his wrath can flare up in a moment. Blessed are all who take refuge in him."   Psalm 2:12

"Blessed are they who keep his statutes and seek him with all their heart."   Psalm 119:2

"Seek the Lord while he may be found; call on him while he is near. Let the wicked forsake his way and the evil man his thoughts. Let him turn to the Lord, and he will have mercy on him, and to our God, for he will freely pardon."   Isaiah 55: 6-7

"The Lord is with you when you are with him. If you seek him, he will be found by you, but if you forsake him, he will forsake you."   2 Chronicles 15: 2b

According to the *American Heritage Dictionary,* to for-sake is*:* "To give up (something formerly held dear), alto-gether abandon."

To live a less than perfect life, have doubts or questions about your relationship with God, is not forsaking Him; "... for all have sinned and fall short of the glory of God..." (Romans 3: 23) Continue to seek Jesus, God's Son, with all your heart. Come to Him. It is a matter of life or death!

"The Father loves the Son and has placed everything in his hands. Whoever believes in the Son has eternal life, but who-ever rejects the Son will not see life, for God's wrath remains on him."   John 3: 35-36

"Then Jesus declared, "I am the bread of life. He who comes to me will never go hungry, and he who believes in me will never be thirsty. But as I told you, you have seen me and still you do not believe. All that the Father gives me will come to me, and whoever comes to me I will never drive away."   John 6: 35-37

"For I have come down from heaven not to do my will but to do the will of him who sent me. And this is the will of him who sent me, that I shall lose none of all that he has given me, but raise them up at the last day. For my Father's will is that everyone who looks to the Son and believes in him shall have eternal life, and I will raise him up at the last day."   John 6: 38-40

*"Let us join with each other in oneness of
Body, soul, spirit, and mind."*

Have you ever been so excited about being with someone special, that you simply cannot contain your excitement or emotions? Simultaneously, your body, soul, spirit and mind engage in overwhelming desire to meet that person, who-ever they may be. Your adrenaline is flowing wildly as you meet, and you joyfully share your love for each other. If mere human emotions can evoke such a joyous response, just imaging the unspeakable joy of meeting Jesus—face to face. So, look to Jesus and believe in Him; love Him whole-heartedly, and bask in His never-ending flow of return love, right now.

"Father, I want those you have given me to be with me where I am, and to see my glory, the glory you have given me because you loved me before the creation of the world."
John 17: 24

"...I have loved you with an everlasting love; I have drawn you with loving-kindness."   Jeremiah 31:3

"Love the Lord you God with all your heart and with all your soul and with all your strength."   Deuteronomy 6:5

"But if from there you seek the Lord your God, you will find him if you look for him with all your heart and with all your soul."   Deuteronomy 4: 29

"I pray that out of his glorious riches he may strengthen you with power through his Spirit in your inner being, so that Christ may dwell in your hearts through faith. And I pray that you, being rooted and established in love, may have power, together with all the saints, to grasp how wide and long and high and deep is the love of Christ, and to know this love that surpasses knowledge—that you may be filled to the measure of all the fullness of God."   Ephesians 3: 16-19

Just imagine, being loved by God Almighty, beyond human understanding. The phrase, "Jesus loves you," is a very powerful statement—not simply a cliché.

"And the peace of God, which transcends all understanding, will guard your hearts and your minds in Christ Jesus."

Philippians 4:7

"For God so loved the world that he gave his one and only Son, that whoever believes in him shall not perish but have eternal life. For God did not send his Son into the world to condemn the world, but to save the world through him. Whoever believes in him is not condemned, but whoever does not believe stands condemned already because he has not believed in the name of God's one and only Son."

John 3:16-18

"As obedient children, do not conform to the evil desires you had when you lived in ignorance. But just as he who called you is holy, so be holy in all you do; for it is written: "Be holy because I am holy." 1 Peter 1: 14-16

"Who may stand in his holy place? He who has clean hands and a pure heart, who does not lift up his soul to an idol or swear by what is false. He will receive a blessing from the Lord and vindication from God his Savior." Psalm 24: 3b-5

Chapter Six

A Clean Slate

In an effort to restore your home to its original beauty, you clean it to remove dirt, dust and debris. To prevent sickness, you purify your drinking water. You may have worked meticulously, thinking that you cleaned the whole house, and have purified the water; but, did you really clean every square inch of the house, and remove every impurity from the water? Most likely, a white glove test will show some residual dirt was left behind; also, if you test your drinking water, it probably will contain some impurities. The words "clean," "pure," and "whole," are frequently used words, which usually miss the mark of their true meanings.

You house may appear spotless and clean, and your water may be drinkable, but only God can truly cleanse, purify, and achieve wholeness. Sin in your life, like the dirt and the impurities, makes you miss the mark of living according to God's standards. Fear not. With God all things are possible. He can make you clean, pure and whole; but, the decision is up to you.

Have you asked Jesus to cleanse you from your sins? Don't fear coming to Him. He already knows what your sins are, and will never turn you away.

"Pure are you in My sight. For I have cleansed you Myself.
You are pure and whole with Me. Don't be afraid."

"In my anguish I cried to the Lord, and he answered by setting me free. The Lord is with me; I will not be afraid."
Psalm 118: 5-6a

"All that the Father gives me will come to me, and whoever comes to me I will never drive away."   John 6:37

"Search me, O God, and know my heart; test me and know my anxious thoughts. See if there is any offensive way in me, and lead me in the way everlasting."   Psalm 139: 23-24

"O Lord, you have searched me and you know me. You know when I sit and when I rise; you perceive my thoughts from afar. You discern my going out and my lying down; you are familiar with all my ways."   Psalm 139: 1-3

"If we claim to be without sin, we deceive ourselves and the truth is not in us. If we confess our sins, he is faithful and just and will forgive us our sins and purify us from all unrighteousness."   1 John 1: 8-9

"Have mercy on me, O God, according to your unfailing love; according to your great compassion blot out my transgressions. Wash away all my iniquity and cleanse me from my sin. For I know my transgressions, and my sin is always before me. Against you, you only, have I sinned..."
Palm 139: 1- 4a

"Pure are you in my sight, for I have cleansed you Myself."

"Create in me a pure heart, O God, and renew a steadfast spirit within me. Do not cast me from your presence or take your Holy Spirit from me. Restore to me the joy of your salvation and grant me a willing spirit to sustain me."

Psalm 51: 10-12

If you are truly sorry for your sins, confess them to Jesus, and know that He will forgive you, you will be made pure and whole in His sight. A great exchange will take place in your life. When you give your sins to Jesus, in exchange, He will cleanse you with His precious blood, and impart unto you His righteousness.

"We implore you on Christ's behalf: Be reconciled to God. God made him who had no sin to be sin for us, so that in him we might become the righteousness of God."

2 Corinthians 5: 20b-21

"In him we have redemption through his blood, the forgiveness of sins, in accordance with the riches of God's grace that he lavished on us with all wisdom and understanding."

Ephesians 1: 7-8

"For he chose us in him before the foundation of the world to be holy and blameless in his sight. In love he predestined us to be adopted as his sons through Jesus Christ, in accordance with his pleasure and will—to the praise of his glorious grace, which he has freely given us in the One he loves."

Ephesians 1: 4-6

Remaining in a sinful state and having a right relationship with God is impossible. Nonetheless, with God all things are possible. To show us His great, unmatchable love, and to reconcile us (bring us back) into a right relationship with God, Jesus paid the price for our sins with His precious blood, on the Cross of Calvary.

"For God was pleased to have all his fullness dwell in him, and through him to reconcile to himself all things, whether things on earth or things in heaven, by making peace through his blood, shed on the cross."　　　　　Colossians 1: 19-20

"You are pure and whole with Me. Don't be afraid."

"Once you were alienated from God and were enemies in your minds because of your evil behavior. But now he has reconciled you by Christ's physical body through death to present you holy in his sight, without blemish and free from accusation—if you continue in your faith, established and firm, not moved from the hope held out in the Gospel."
　　　　　　　　　　　　　　　　　Colossians 1: 21-23a

"Fear not, for I have redeemed you; I have summoned you by name; you are mine."
　　　　　　　　　　　　　　　　　Isaiah 43: 1b

Jesus is calling your name. Will you be reconciled, and come back to Him?

"As God's fellow workers, we urge you not to receive God's grace in vain. For he says, "In the time of my favor I heard you, and in the day of salvation I helped you." I tell you, now is the time of God's favor, now is the day of salvation."
　　　　　　　　　　　　　　　　　2 Corinthians 6:1-2

God says, "now"—Today, is the day of salvation. When we go to bed at night, we close our eyes, thinking we'll wake up in the morning, tomorrow. We may have laid out our plans for "tomorrow;" yet, in the morning, when we wake up—if it is God's will that we do wake up, somehow, it is today again. You see, tomorrow never really comes. So, since you don't know what the next day may bring, won't you come to Jesus today, while you still have time?

"Now listen you who say, "Today or tomorrow we will go to this or that city, spend a year there, carry on business and make money. Why, you do not even know what will happen tomorrow. What is your life? You are a mist that appears for a little while and then vanishes. Instead, you ought to say, "If it is the Lord's will, we will live and do this or that." As it is, you boast and brag. All such boasting is evil. Anyone, then, who knows the good he ought to do and doesn't do it, sins."

James 4: 13-17

Are you ready and willing to do the good thing you ought to do, while it is still today, and you are still able? Jesus is calling you.

"Here I am! I stand at the door and knock. If anyone hears my voice and opens the door, I will come in and eat with him, and he with me.   Revelation 3:20

"Therefore, God again set a certain day, calling it Today, when a long time later he spoke through David, as was said before: "Today, if you hear his voice, do not harden your hearts."   Hebrews 4:7

Jesus is waiting for you to heed His call. Come to Him, just as you are.

"You are pure and whole with Me. Don't be afraid."

"All that the Father gives me will come to me, and whoever comes to me I will never drive away."

John 6:37

"You see, at just the right time, when we were still powerless, Christ died for the ungodly. Very rarely will anyone die for a righteous man, though for a good man someone might possibly dare to die. But God demonstrates his own love for us in this: While we were still sinners, Christ died for us."

Romans 5: 6-8

Jesus Christ died on the cross to save us from our sins — while we were still sinners. What a loving and gracious Savior we have. He not only paid the penalty for our sins, but also, He removed the guilt of our sins. Have you ever confessed the same sin over and over, after He has already forgiven you? Sometimes we find it difficult to forgive ourselves; however, we must accept His forgiveness and put our sins behind us.

We have this great privilege, because Jesus declared us not guilty — justified. Being freed from sin and its guilt, we can move forward in our walk with Christ.

"...But one thing I do: Forgetting what is behind and straining toward what is ahead, I press on toward the goal to win the prize for which God has called me heavenward in Christ Jesus."   Philippians 3: 13b-14

"There is no difference, for all have sinned and fall short of the glory of God, and are justified freely by his grace through the redemption that came by Christ Jesus. God presented him as a sacrifice of atonement, through faith in his blood."

Romans 3: 22b-25a

"He was delivered over to death for our sins and was raised to life for our justification. Therefore, since we have been justified through faith, we have peace with God through our Lord Jesus Christ, through whom we have gained access by faith into this grace in which we now stand. And we rejoice in the hope of the glory of God."   Romans 4:25— 5: 1-2

"Since we now have been justified by his blood, how much more shall we be saved from God's wrath through him! For if, when we were God's enemies, we were reconciled to him through the death of his Son, how much more, having been reconciled, shall we be saved through his life!"

Romans 5: 9-10

"For I have cleansed you Myself. You are pure and whole with Me.
Don't be afraid."

So, are you still carrying around a load of guilt, unnecessarily? If you asked for forgiveness, the Lord God Almighty already forgave you, and buried your sins in the sea of forgetfulness. Who are you not to forgive yourself?

"Who is a God like you, who pardons sin and forgives the transgression of the remnant of his inheritance? You do not stay angry forever but delight to show mercy. You will again have compassion on us; you will tread our sins underfoot and hurl all our iniquities into the depths of the sea."

Micah 7: 18-19

"I, even I, am he who blots out your transgressions, for my own sake, and remembers your sins no more." Isaiah 43:25

Praise and thank the Lord for His great mercy and compassion. Rejoice! Do not be afraid. His unending love for you never grows cold.

Chapter Seven

No Fear: Eternally His

"Fear not, I will be with you always; we are one, never to part.
My love for you never ends."

"Fear not, for I have redeemed you; I have summoned you by name; you are mine. When you pass through the waters, I will be with you; and when you pass through the rivers, they will not sweep over you. When you walk through the fire, you will not be burned; the flames will not set you ablaze. For I am the Lord, your God, the Holy One of Israel, your Savior."   Isaiah 43: 1b-3a

"Do not be afraid, for I am with you…"   Isaiah 43: 5a

"I said, 'you are my servant'; I have chosen you and have not rejected you. So do not fear, for I am with you; do not be dismayed, for I am your God. I will strengthen you and help you; I will uphold you with my righteous right hand."
                                                           Isaiah 41: 9b-10

God promises to strengthen us, and uphold us with His righteous right hand. Unfortunately, sometimes we forget about His promises, and try to solve our problems in our own strength and power. Instead of depending on fallible, human means, we must trust Him enough to rest securely in His promises to help, and not be afraid of the outcome. By becoming one with Christ, through the power of the Holy Spirit, His power and His strength will get us through any situation.

"'Not by might nor by power, but by my Spirit', says the Lord Almighty."   Zechariah 4:6b

"We are one, never to part."

The promise of being one with Jesus, through the power of the Holy Spirit, is reserved for believers. The "world"—people who may know of Jesus, but have no personal relationship with Him, cannot claim this promise, without claiming Jesus as their personal Savior.

"If you love me, you will obey what I command. And I will ask the Father, and he will give you another Counselor to be with you forever—the Spirit of truth."   John 14: 15-17a

"The world cannot accept him, because it neither sees him nor knows him. But you know him, for he lives with you and will be in you. I will not leave you as orphans; I will come to you."   John 14: 17b-18

Since God Himself tells us that He will not leave us as "orphans," and that He will, "come to us," if we welcome Him into our hearts, we have Christ in us, "the hope of glory."

"To them God has chosen to make known among the Gentiles the glorious riches of this mystery, which is Christ in you, the hope of glory."   Colossians 1:27

"For in Christ all the fullness of the Deity lives in bodily form, and you have been given fullness in Christ, who is the head over every power and authority."   Colossians 2: 9-10

When we become one with Jesus Christ, we become, "new creations." People should see the nature of Jesus in us, not our old sinful nature, because we are His representatives to the world.

"Therefore, if anyone is in Christ, he is a new creation; the old has gone, the new has come!"   2 Corinthians 5:17

"All this is from God, who reconciled us to himself through Christ and gave us the ministry of reconciliation: that God was reconciling the world to himself in Christ, not counting men's sins against them. And he has committed to us the message of reconciliation."   2 Corinthians 5: 18-19

"We are therefore Christ's ambassadors, as though God were making his appeal through us. We implore you on Christ's behalf: Be reconciled to God. God made him who had no sin to be sin for us, so that in him we might become the righteousness of God."   2 Corinthians 5: 20-21

Just as a skilled surgeon would remove a poisonous, gangrenous limb from our body to save our life, Jesus will perform a type of "spiritual surgery" on our hearts, if we allow. By using the power of God, He helps us put our old, sinful natures to death, so we can be alive in Christ, and live for Him.

"In him you were also circumcised, in the putting off of the sinful nature, not with a circumcision done by hands of men, but with the circumcision done by Christ, having been buried with him in baptism and raised with him in your faith in the power of God, who raised him from the dead."

Colossians 2: 11-12

"When you were dead in your sins and in the uncircumcision of your sinful nature, God made you alive with Christ. He forgave us all our sins…"

Colossians 2:13

"So then, just as you received Christ Jesus as Lord, continue to live in him, rooted and built up in him, strengthened in the faith as you were taught, and overflowing with thankfulness."

Colossians 2: 6-7

"I have been crucified with Christ and I no longer live, but Christ lives in me. The life I live in the body, I live by faith in the Son of God, who loved me and gave himself for me."

Galatians 2: 20

"We are one, never to part."

What a glorious day it will be when we realize our oneness with God.

"On that day you will realize that I am in my Father, and you are in me, and I am in you."

John 14:20

"Whoever has my commands and obeys them, he is the one who loves me. He who loves me will be loved by my Father, and I too will love him and show myself to him."

John 14:21

"We are one, never to part. My love for you never ends."

"I have drawn you with an everlasting love; I have drawn you with loving- kindness." Jeremiah 31: 3b

"If anyone acknowledges that Jesus is the Son of God, God lives in him and he in God. And so we know and rely on the love God has for us. God is love. Whoever lives in love lives in God, and God in him. In this way, love is made complete among us so that we will have confidence on the day of judgment, because in this world we are like him." 1 John 4: 15-17

"There is no fear in love. But perfect love drives out fear, because fear has to do with punishment. The one who fears is not made perfect in love. We love because he first loved us." 1 John 4: 18-19

In Psalm 136: 1-26 the phrase *"His love endures forever"* is repeated after each and every verse. For example: "Give thanks to the Lord, for he is good, *His love endures forever."* Psalm 136:1

"Give thanks to the God of gods. *His love endures forever."* Psalm 136: 2

On and on throughout this beautiful Psalm, the Psalmist reiterates the wonderful promise of God's enduring love, that never ends. This promise is like a golden thread that runs throughout the Bible, continually reminding us of God's enduring love for us that never ends.

"Give thanks to the Lord, for he is good; his love endures forever. Cry out, "Save us O God our Savior…"" 1 Chronicles 16: 34-35a

"The trumpeters and singers joined in unison, as with one voice, to give praise and thanks to the Lord. Accompanied by trumpets, cymbals, and other instruments, they raised their voices in praise to the Lord and sang: "He is good; his love endures forever." 2 Chronicles 5:13a

God is continually extending His love. He is reaching down from Heaven in love, desiring to take your hand. As a bridegroom "takes the hand" of his bride, to be one with her, until death do they part, Jesus is seeking your hand, in an eternal love relationship with Him. How will you respond?

Chapter Eight

Forever His

"Come, come, come unto Me; take My hand. You are Mine forever: Come."

It seems as if God uses the tool of repetition to drive important points home. For instance, in this portion of *Love-Letter*, the word, *"come"* is used four times. Additionally, throughout the entire *Love- Letter from Jesus,* the word *"come"* is used ten times. Don't you think that God is trying to make a point?

"Then Jesus declared, " I am the bread of life. He who comes to me will never go hungry, and he who believes in me will never be thirsty."   John 6:35

"...Jesus stood and said in a loud voice, "If anyone is thirsty, let him come to me and drink. Whoever believes in me, as the Scripture has said, streams of living water will flow from within him." By this he meant the Spirit, whom those who believed in him were later to receive."   John 7: 37b-39a

"All that the Father gives me will come to me, and whoever comes to me I will never drive away." John 6:37

"Come to me, all you who are weary and burdened, and I will give you rest. Take my yoke upon you and learn from me, for I am gentle and humble in heart, and you will find rest for your souls. For my yoke is easy and my burden is light."   Matthew 11:28-30

"Turn to me and be saved, all you ends of the earth; for I am God, and there is no other."   Isaiah 45:22

Have you come to Jesus to be saved? What a precious and priceless invitation He gives us. Not only will He save us and give us assurance of eternal life, He will also be with us to hold our hand, give us strength, and guide us throughout life—forever.

"Take My hand. You are Mine forever; Come."

"Yet I am always with you; you hold me by my right hand. You guide me with your counsel, and afterward you will take me into glory. Whom have I in heaven but you? And earth has nothing I desire besides you. My flesh and my heart may fail, but God is the strength of my heart and my portion forever."   Psalm 73: 23-26

"Those who are far from you will perish; you destroy all who are unfaithful to you. But as for me, it is good to be near God. I have made the Sovereign Lord my refuge; I will tell of all your deeds."   Psalm 73: 27-28

"I love you, O Lord, my strength. The Lord is my rock, my fortress and my deliverer; my God is my rock, in whom I take refuge. He is my shield and the horn of my salvation, my stronghold." Psalm 18:1-2

"Because you are my help, I sing in the shadow of your wings. My soul clings to you; your right hand upholds me." Psalm 63: 7-8

Unfortunately, we live in a very perilous world. Peace and security, where it seems to exist, is very superficial and fragile. Fear of the unknown seems to lurk around every corner of life. Fortunately, by coming to Jesus, we can allow Him, God Almighty, to be our rock, fortress, deliverer, and stronghold. Even though we are weak and powerless in our own strength, when we walk hand in hand with God, He protects us with His strength, He hears our cries, and gives us victory.

"The cords of death entangled me; the torrents of destruction overwhelmed me. The cords of the grave coiled around me; the snares of death confronted me. In my distress I called to the Lord; I cried to my God for help. From his temple he heard my voice; my cry came before him, into his ears." Psalm 18: 4-6

"He parted the heavens and came down; dark clouds were under his feet." Psalm 18:9

"He reached down from on high and took hold of me; he drew me out of deep waters. He rescued me from my powerful enemy, from my foes, who were too strong for me. They confronted me in the day of my disaster, but the Lord was my support. He brought me out into a spacious place; he rescued me because he delighted in me." Psalm 18: 16-19

"He is my loving God and my fortress, my stronghold and my deliverer, my shield, in whom I take refuge, who subdues people under me. O Lord, what is man that you care for him, the son of man that you think of him? Man is like a breath; his days are like a fleeting shadow."   Psalm 144: 2-4

"Come unto Me. Take My hand."

"Reach down from on high; deliver me and rescue me from the mighty waters, from the hands of foreigners whose mouths are full of lies, whose right hands are deceitful."
                                                    Psalm 144: 7-8

Satan—the Devil, is a murderer, a liar, a cheater, and a deceiver.

"He was a murderer from the beginning, not holding to the truth, for there is no truth in him. When he lies, he speaks his native language, for he is a liar and the father of lies."
                                                    John 8: 44b

"Be self- controlled and alert. Your enemy the devil prowls around like a roaring lion looking for someone to devour. Resist him, standing firm in the faith."   1 Peter 5:8-9a

"And the God of all grace, who called you to his eternal glory in Christ, after you have suffered a little while, will himself restore you and make you strong, firm and steadfast. To him be the power forever and ever. Amen."
                                                    1 Peter 5: 10-11

Jesus is our ultimate source of truth and life. In fact, He is the truth and the life. Accepting Him as our Savior, and standing firm and steadfast in our faith, is our only way to resist Satan, and to have true freedom and eternal life.

"Jesus answered, "I am the way and the truth and the life. No one comes to the Father except through me."   John 14:6

"If you hold to my teaching, you are really my disciples. Then you will know the truth, and the truth will set you free."   John 8:31b

"Jesus replied, "I tell you the truth, everyone who sins is a slave to sin. Now a slave has no permanent place in the family, but a son belongs to it forever. So if the Son sets you free, you will be free indeed."   John 8: 34-36

Freedom! Most of us like the sound of that word. Many would have given up everything for freedom. Just imagine, Jesus gives us freedom as a gift! Would you like to be free in Christ Jesus, and have a permanent place in His family? You can be. As He reaches down to you, won't you reach up to Him? Give up your sinful ways, and allow Him to give you freedom, by giving you victory over sin, salvation and eternal life.

"Jesus replied, "I tell you the truth, everyone who sins is a slave to sin. Now a slave has no permanent place in the family, but a son belongs to it forever. So if the Son sets you free, you will be free indeed."   John 8: 34-36

"What a wretched man I am! Who will rescue me from this body of death? Thanks be to God—through Jesus Christ our Lord! So then, I myself in my mind am a slave to God's law, but in the sinful nature a slave to the law of sin."
                                                                            Romans 7: 24-25

"Therefore, there is now no condemnation for those who are in Christ Jesus, because through Christ Jesus the law of the Spirit of life set me free from the law of sin and death."

Romans 8: 1-2

"For what the law was powerless to do in that it was weakened by the sinful nature, God did by sending his own Son in the likeness of sinful man to be a sin offering. And so he condemned sin in sinful man, in order that the righteous requirements of the law might be fully met in us, who do not live according to the sinful nature but according to the Spirit."

Romans 8: 3-4

"For the perishable must clothe itself with the imperishable, and the mortal with immortality. When the perishable has been clothed with the imperishable, and the mortal with immortality, then the saying that is written will come true: "Death has been swallowed up in victory."

1 Corinthians 15: 53-54

"Where, O death, is your victory? Where, O death, is your sting? The sting of death is sin, and the power of sin is the law. But thanks be to God! He gives us the victory through our Lord Jesus Christ."

1 Corinthians 15: 55-57

"Therefore, my dear brothers, stand firm. Let nothing move you." 1 Corinthians 15: 58a

Earthly victories are fragile, are subject to change, and can fade over time; conversely, by remaining firm in our faith in Jesus, He will give us victory that can remain permanent and unchangeable.

"...but because Jesus lives forever, he has a permanent priesthood. Therefore he is able to save completely those who come to God through him, because he always lives to intercede for them."

Hebrews 7:24-25

"Jesus Christ is the same yesterday and today and forever."

Hebrews 13:8

"...for everyone born of God overcomes the world. This is the victory that has overcome the world, even our faith. Who is it that overcomes the world? Only he who believes that Jesus is the Son of God."   1 John 5: 4-5

"Take My hand; you are Mine forever."

Jesus extends His invitation of love and forgiveness of sins, to every person in the world, even to those yet unborn. Since His invitation extends to you personally, would you like to be His forever and bask in His love? He loves you so much; won't you love Him back? Take His hand, Come.

"Kiss the Son, lest He be angry and you be destroyed in your way, for his wrath can flare up in a moment. Blessed are all who take refuge in him."   Psalm 2:12

A kiss is usually recognized as a sign of love or respect. Are you ready to "Kiss the Son," Jesus, and love Him as He loves you?

Chapter Nine

Reflections of His Love

"Love me as I have loved you" is a powerful state-ment. Jesus does not give us an option to love; He commands our love.

"Love Me as I have loved you."

"As the Father has loved me, so have I loved you. Now remain in my love. If you obey my commands, you will remain in my love, just as I have obeyed my Father's com-mands and remain in his love. I have told you this so that my joy may be in you and that your joy may be complete. My command is this: Love each other as I have loved you."

John 15:9-12

"Jesus replied: " 'Love the Lord your God with all your heart and with all your soul and with all your mind.' This is the first and greatest commandment. And the second is like it: 'Love your neighbor as yourself.'"   Matthew 22: 37-39

"We love because he first loved us. If anyone says, "I love God," yet hates his brother, he is a liar. For anyone who does not love his brother, whom he has seen, cannot love God, whom he has not seen. And he has given us this command: Whoever loves God must also love his brother."

1 John 4: 19-21

How can we love God and our "brother" (all mankind) as He loves us? In our own power we simply can't. Human love is imperfect, weak, selfish, and fickle. Fortunately, for the believer, the Holy Spirit provides power to love God and others, as He commands.

"I pray that out of his glorious riches he may strengthen you with power through his Spirit in your inner being, so that Christ may dwell in your hearts thought faith. And I pray that you, being rooted and established in love, may have power, together with all the saints, to grasp how wide and long and high and deep is the love of Christ, and to know this love that surpasses knowledge—that you may be filled to the measure of all the fullness of God."   Ephesians 3: 16-19

"Now to him who is able to do immeasurably more than all we ask or imagine, according to his power that is at work within us, to him be the glory in the church and in Christ Jesus throughout all generations, forever and ever! Amen."

Ephesians 3: 20-21

Since we can't rely on our own strength, and we can rely on the power of the Holy Spirit, we have the glorious privilege to reflect God's love to others, by treating them as we would want to be treated. Since we are all created in the image of God, we must treat each person as if he or she were Christ himself.

"So God created man on his own image, in the image of God he created him; male and female he created them."
Genesis 1: 27

"The King will reply, 'I tell you the truth, whatever you did for one of the least of these brothers of mine, you did for me.'"
Matthew 25:40

"He will reply, 'I tell you the truth, whatever you did not do for one of the least of these, you did not do for me.'"
Matthew 25:45

"Is not this the kind of fasting I have chosen...? Is it not to share your for with the hungry and to provide the poor wanderer with shelter—when you see the naked, to clothe him, and not to turn away from your own flesh and blood? Then your light will break forth like the dawn, and your healing will quickly appear; then your righteousness will go before you, and the glory of the Lord will be your rear guard."
Isaiah 58: 6a, 7-8

A mirror faithfully reflects the exact image of the object placed in front of it. Although the mirror has no power of its own, with the presence of light, the image can be reflected and seen. Without the presence of light—in darkness, no image can be reflected or seen. Since we are created in God's image, and Jesus (God) is the "Light of the world," (John 8:12) it is imperative that we reflect His light and love.

"When Jesus spoke again to the people, he said, "I am the light of the world. Whoever follows me will never walk in darkness, but will have the light of life."
John 8:12

"This is the message we have heard from him and declare to you: God is light; in him there is no darkness at all."

1 John 1:5

"If we claim to have fellowship with him yet walk in the darkness, we lie and do not live by the truth. But if we walk in the light, as he is in the light, we have fellowship with one another, and the blood of Jesus, his Son, purifies us from all sin."

1 John 1: 6-7

"For God, who said, "let light shine out of darkness," made his light shine in our hearts to give us the light of the knowledge of the glory of God in the face of Christ. But we have this treasure in jars of clay to show that this all-surpassing power is from God and not from us."   2 Corinthians 4: 6-7

"Love Me as I have loved you."

Who, but The God of Love: Jesus Christ, would give mere human beings ("jars of clay"), the light of the knowledge of the glory of God? He does this so we can emulate Him, by allowing His light to shine from us, reflecting His love to all mankind.

"God is love. Whoever lives in love lives in God, and God in him. In this way, love is made complete among us so that we will have confidence on the day of judgment, because in this world we are like him. There is no fear in love. But perfect love drives out fear, because fear has to do with punishment."

1 John 4: 16b-18a

"God is love" is a very old and well known phrase; nevertheless, just what is God's definition of love? In 1 Corinthians Chapter 13, sometimes referred to as the "Love

Chapter" by some Christians, God gives us His definition of love.

"Love is patient, love is kind. It does not envy, it does not boast, it is not proud, it is not rude, it is not self-seeking, it is not easily angered, it keeps no record of wrongs. Love does not delight in evil but rejoices with the truth. It always protects, always trusts, always hopes, always perseveres. Love never fails." 1 Corinthians 13: 4-8a

Now that we have God's definition of love in 1 Corinthians 13: 4-8, we can apply it to our lives, and reflect His love to others, starting with virtues of patience and kindness.

"Love is patient, love is kind." 1 Corinthians 13:4a

"Live in peace with each other. And we urge you, brothers, warn those who are idle, encourage the timid, help the weak, be patient with everyone. Make sure that nobody pays back wrong for wrong, but always try to be kind to each other and to everyone else." 1 Thessalonians 5: 13b-15

"Love Me as I have loved you."

"Therefore, as God's chosen people, holy and dearly loved, clothe yourselves with compassion, kindness, humility, gentleness, and patience. Bear with each other and forgive whatever grievances you may have against one another. Forgive as the Lord forgave you. And over all these virtues put on love, which binds them all together in perfect unity." Colossians 3: 12-14

"He who is kind to the poor lends to the Lord, and he will reward him for what he has done."
Proverbs 19:17

"A patient man has great understanding, but a quick-tempered man displays folly."

Proverbs 14:29

Jealousy (envy), can provoke a person to be "quick-tempered and display folly," in a rage of anger. To avoid this pitfall, we need to put God's ideals of love found in 1 Corinthians 13, into practice every day.

"It does not envy." 1 Corinthians 13:4b

"A heart at peace gives life to the body, but envy rots the bones."

Proverbs 14:30

"I hear that there may be quarreling, jealousy, outbursts of anger, factions, slander, gossip, arrogance and disorder."

2 Corinthians 12:20b

"You are still worldly. For since there is jealousy and quarreling among you, are you not worldly?" 1 Corinthians 3:3a

Arrogance, disorder, quarreling, and other such sins usually have their root in the sin of pride. A proud heart and an arrogant spirit contradict God's law of love. 1 Corinthians 13 has much to say about what love is; conversely, it also has much to say about what love is not.

"It is not proud." 1 Corinthians 13:4c

"The Lord detests all the proud of heart. Be sure of they: They will not go unpunished."

Proverbs 16:5

"Pride goes before destruction, a haughty spirit before a fall."

Proverbs 16:18

76

"This is the one I esteem: he who is humble and contrite in spirit, and trembles at my word."   Isaiah 66: 2b

"The Lord is close to the brokenhearted and saves those who are crushed in spirit."   Psalm 34:18

"But, "Let him who boasts boast in the Lord." For it is not the one who commends himself who is approved, but the one whom the Lord commends."   2 Corinthians 10: 17-18

"May I never boast except in the cross of our Lord Jesus Christ…"   Galatians 6:14a

"For it is by grace you have been saved, through faith—and this not from yourselves, it is the gift of God—not by works, so that no one can boast."   Ephesians 2: 8-9

1 Corinthians 13:5 has much more to speak about, concerning what love is not.

"It is not rude, it is not self-seeking, it is not easily angered, it keeps no record of wrongs."   1 Corinthians 13:5

"Love Me as I have loved you."

When Jesus died on the cross to save us from our sins, He knew he would suffer terribly; yet, He was not rude to his accusers. He humbly endured the suffering that we should have endured—the utmost, selfless, act of love; furthermore, He forgave His accusers.

"What shall I do, then, with Jesus who is called Christ?" Pilate asked. They all answered, "Crucify him!" "Why? What crime has he committed?" Pilate asked. But they shouted all the louder, "Crucify him!"   Matthew 27: 22-23

"Then he released Barabbas to them. But he had Jesus flogged, and handed him over to be crucified."

Matthew 27:26

"Then the governor's soldiers took Jesus into the Praetorium and gathered the whole company of soldiers around him. They stripped him and put a scarlet robe on him, and then twisted together a crown of thorns and set it on his head. They put a staff in his right hand and knelt in front of him and mocked him. "Hail, king of the Jews!" they said. They spit on him, and took the staff and struck him on the head again and again. After they had mocked him, they took off the robe and put his own clothes on him. Then they led him away to crucify him." Matthew 27: 27-31

"When they came to the place called the Skull, there they crucified him, along with the criminals—one on his right, the other on his left. Jesus said, "Father, forgive them, for they do not know what they are doing." Luke 23: 33-34a

"One of the criminals who hung there hurled insults at him: "Aren't you the Christ? Save yourself and us!" But the other criminal rebuked him. "Don't you fear God, he said, "since you are under the same sentence? We are punished justly, for we are getting what our deeds deserve. But this man has done nothing wrong." Luke 23: 39-41

"Then he said, "Jesus, remember me when you come into your kingdom." Jesus answered him, "I tell you the truth, today you will be with me in paradise."   Luke 23 42-43

"Love Me as I have loved you."

"Greater love has no one than this, that he lay down his life for his friends."   John 15:13

"I am the good shepherd. The good shepherd lays down his life for the sheep." John 10:11

Jesus gave us the ultimate gift of love, when He died on the cross to save us from our sins. He took no delight in the evil, shameful, circumstances of the crucifixion. However, he did delight and rejoice in the truth, that He was the only One who could change the course of sinful mankind from eternal condemnation—hell, to eternal life in Heaven. His precious free gift of Salvation is available to every person that accepts Jesus as Lord and Savior. Have you accepted Jesus, and His ultimate gift of eternal life?

"Love does not delight in evil but rejoices with the truth." 1 Corinthians 13:6

"Woe to them who call evil good and good evil..."
Isaiah 5: 20a

"You are not a God who takes pleasure in evil; with you the wicked cannot dwell." Psalm 5:4

"This is the verdict: Light has come into the world, but men loved darkness instead of light because their deeds were evil. Everyone who does evil hates the light, and will not come into the light for fear that his deeds will be exposed. But whoever lives by the truth comes into the light, so that it may be seen plainly that what he has done has been done through God." John 3: 19-21

"I have no greater joy than to hear that my children are walking in the truth." 3 John 4

"Jesus answered, "I am the way and the truth and the life. No one comes to the Father except through me." John 14:6

Have you rejoiced in the One (Jesus), who is "The Truth?" Have you rejoiced in Jesus as your Savior, and Protector, the One in whom you can place all your hope and trust?

1 Corinthians 13 continues to speak of God's ideals of love.

"It always protects, always trusts, always hopes, always perseveres." 1 Corinthians 13: 7

Love protects: "Do not withhold your mercy from me, O Lord; may your love and your truth always protect me." Psalm 40:11

Love Trusts: "Do not let your hearts be troubled. Trust in God; trust also in me." John 14:1

Love Hopes: "But since we belong to the day, let us be self-controlled, putting on faith and love as a breastplate, and the hope of salvation as a helmet." 1 Thessalonians 5:8

"The Lord is good to those whose hope is in him, to the one who seeks him; it is good to wait quietly for the salvation of the Lord." Lamentations 3: 25-26

"...the mystery that has been kept hidden for ages and generations, but is now disclosed to the saints. To them God has chosen to make known among the Gentiles the glorious riches of this mystery, which is Christ in you, the hope of glory." Colossians 1: 26-27

Love Perseveres: "But one thing I do: Forgetting what is behind and straining toward what is ahead, I press on toward the goal to win the prize for which God has called me heavenward in Christ Jesus." Philippians 3: 13b-14

"Consider it pure joy, my brothers, whenever you face trials of many kinds, because you know that the testing of your faith develops perseverance. Perseverance must finish its work so that you may be mature and complete, not lacking anything."   James 1: 2-4

"May the Lord direct your hearts into God's love, and Christ's perseverance."   2 Thessalonians 3:5

"Blessed is the man who perseveres under trial, because when he has stood the test, he will receive the crown of life that God has promised to those who love him."   James 1:12

Peoples' true characters are best measured by how they react to unexpected situations, every day problems, and catastrophic events. Guided with God's wisdom, and armed with His strength, they can successfully persevere through any trial, and grow in strength and character. (Become "mature and complete").

In contrast, those who react to adverse events depending on impulsive, self-serving interests, rarely succeed in the eyes of God. Human wisdom and strength falls short of God's standards. They may gain a feeling of self satisfaction, accomplishment, or worldly success, but, all too often they hurt themselves and others in their pursuit. "Pride goes before destruction, a haughty spirit before a fall."

Proverbs 16:18

1 Corinthians 13:8a ends with three of the most powerful words: "Love never fails."

"But the eyes of the Lord are on those who fear him, on those whose hope is in his unfailing love, to deliver them from death and keep them alive in famine." Psalm 33: 18-19

"Because of the Lord's great love we are not consumed, for his compassions never fail. They are new every morning; great is your faithfulness." Lamentations 3:22-23

"May your unfailing love rest upon us, O Lord, even as we put our hope in you."   Psalm 33:22

"But I trust in your unfailing love; my heart rejoices in your salvation."   Psalm 13:5

Do you trust in His unfailing love, and rejoice in His Salvation? Jesus is reaching out to you, and would like you to be His forever. He invites you to come. RSVP required. How will you respond?

Chapter Ten

R. S. V. P.

"You are Mine forever: Come."

Most of us have received, and responded to various invitations throughout our lives. Perhaps you were invited to a family reunion, a wedding, or some other special event. Each invitation was from a different source, was for a different event, and was for a particular person or persons. However, Jesus, the One true Source, invites everyone to participate in the same glorious event–Salvation, and eternal life in Heaven with Him. But remember, just being invited to an event doesn't mean you have arrived. You must first respond properly and go to the event; then you will be graciously welcomed. Will you choose to accept Jesus' invitation, and live eternally (forever) in Heaven with Him? Or, will you choose to reject His offer, and spend eternity in hell—forever separated from God, in ongoing torment day and night, with no second chances, or way to escape? The choice is up to you.

After we physically die, our souls will live forever, either in Heaven or in Hell. Where we want to spend eternity is the glorious choice that God gives us. Your choice is a matter of life or death. How will you respond to Jesus' invitation? Choose life; choose Jesus. RSVP required.

"And I saw the dead, great and small, standing before the throne, and books were opened. Another book was opened, which is the book of life."   Revelation 20:12a

Praise the Lord, that He gives us time on Earth, to choose to have our names written into the Lamb's Book of Life, penned with the precious blood of Jesus.

"Nothing impure will ever enter it, nor will anyone who does what is shameful or deceitful, but only those whose names are written in the Lamb's book of life."   Revelation 21:27

"The Father loves the Son and has placed everything in his hands. Whoever believes in the Son has eternal life, but whoever rejects the Son will not see life, for God's wrath remains on him."   John 3: 35-36

"For God so loved the world that he gave his one and only Son, that whoever believes in him shall not perish but have eternal life. For God did not send his Son into the world to condemn the world, but to save the world, through him."
                                                 John 3: 16-17

"Whoever believes in him is not condemned, but whoever does not believe stands condemned already because he has not believed in the name of God's one and only Son."
                                                     John 3: 18

Dear reader, you are a part of the "whoever," that these verses refer to. The invitation is for you. How will you respond?

"The Spirit and the bride say, "Come!" And let him who hears say, "Come!" Whoever is thirsty, let him come; and whoever wishes, let him take the free gift of the water of life."   Revelation 22:17

"If we confess our sins, he is faithful and just and will forgive us our sins, and purify us from all unrighteousness."
                                                                                    1 John 1:9

Why not graciously receive Him right now, by faith.

"That if you confess with your mouth, "Jesus is Lord," and believe in your heart that God raised him from the dead, you will be saved. For it is with your heart that you believe and are justified, and it is with your mouth that you confess and are saved."   Romans 10: 9-10

"Yet to all who received him, to those who believed in his name, he gave the right to become children of God—children not born of natural descent, nor of human decision, or of a husband's will, but born of God." John 1:12-13

Won't you invite Jesus into your heart as your Lord and Savior, join the family of God, and enjoy eternal Salvation? Today is the day of Salvation. Tomorrow is promised to no one.

Jesus is affectionately pleading with you:

"My heart yearns to be with you. Come, come, come unto Me. Take My hand, come. Come close, closer, even closer. Bare yourself before Me, don't be ashamed. You are pure and whole with Me. Don't be afraid. My love for you never ends. You are Mine, forever. Come"

Come to the Savior.

Conclusion

"My lover spoke and said to me,
    "Arise, my darling,
my beautiful one, and come with me.
See! The winter is past;
    the rains are over and gone.
Flowers appear on the earth;
    The season of singing has come,
the cooing of doves
    is heard in our land.
The fig tree forms its early fruit;
    the blossoming vines spread their fragrance.
Arise, come, my darling;
    my beautiful one, come with me."

Song of Songs 2: 10-13

CPSIA information can be obtained at www.ICGtesting.com
Printed in the USA
LVOW090744090312

272195LV00001B/3/P